Great Wor

Mother Teresa

Renu Saran

ISBN : 978-81-288-2616-9

Publisher : Diamond Pocket Books (P) Ltd.
X-30, Okhla Industrial Area, Phase-II
New Delhi-110020
Phone : 011-41351010, 41351066
Fax : 011-41351010
Edition : 2012
Printed by : Sarasu Printers, Delhi-110043

DIAMOND BOOKS

SMS **New Book** at
9911044500 for Alert

ISBN : 978-81-288-3616-9

© Publisher

Publisher	:	**Diamond Pocket Books (P) Ltd.**
		X-30, Okhla Industrial Area, Phase-II
		New Delhi-110020
Phone	:	011-40712100, 41611861
Fax	:	011-41611866
E-mail	:	sales@dpb.in
Website	:	www.diamondbook.in
Edition	:	2011
Printed by	:	Adarsh Printers, Delhi- 110032

Mother Teresa
By- *Renu Saran*

Contents

1. Introduction 5
2. Birth & Childhood 7
3. Childhood Intelligence 9
4. The Call 10
5. Becoming a Nun 11
6. In Indian Colours 13
7. Became Mother Teresa 15
8. Blessed Blue Bordered Sari 17
9. Indian by Choice 19
10. Swiss Man's Ego Punctured 21
11. Help to Needy 23
12. Feeling Pain of Poor 25
13. Meeting Jawaharlal Nehru 27
14. Home for Lepers 29
15. Determined Mother Teresa 31
16. Mother Praised by Nehru 33
17. Nirmal Hriday 33

18. That Crippled Girl 35
19. Chemistry with Indira Gandhi 37
20. Homes Abroad 39
21. Cleanest & Pious 41
22. Coconut Shell 43
23. Premdaan 44
24. Singapore Incident 45
25. No to Custom Duty 47
26. Old Age Homes 48
27. A Living Legend 49
28. Mother's Prayer 51
29. The Last Voyage 53
30. Missionaries of Charity after Mother Teresa . 54
31. Mother Teresa Memorial House 55
32. Sainthood of Mother Teresa 57
33. Timeline : Mother Teresa 59
34. Poems of Mother Teresa 63

Introduction

None in the twentieth century has touched as many hearts as a simple Albanian-born woman, known universally as Mother Teresa. From her tiny frame exuded an infinite expanse of concern and compassion – offering millions of people a glimpse into a world of perfect dedication to a higher reality. The sacrifices and austerities she endured are incomprehensible to the mind but easily appreciated, admired and adored by the heart; for Mother Teresa it was nothing other than pure love.

Mother Teresa enlightened humanity to an ancient spiritual belief to all which is too rare in the modern world – that the highest form of satisfaction can be achieved on earth through the selfless service of the God in humanity. Indeed, she said, she saw everyone, she served as Jesus and through her love of God, expanded her love for humanity.

Day in and day out, Mother Teresa gave herself to the poor, destitute and unloved with an unwavering strength and spirit borne

of her intense life of spiritual disciple. She was the practical embodiment of the perfect disciple of Christ serving Jesus sleeplessly and breathlessly, but without a trace of pride, feeling that her Jesus was a Hindus' Krishna or a Muslims' Mohammad.

Few, in history, have served the neglected classes of humanity with as much zeal as Mother Teresa. She has reminded all of us that none can be left behind if we truly want to achieve a society and world of perfect peace and harmony.

Birth & Childhood

Agnes Gonxha Bojaxhiu, popularly known as Mother Teresa was born on August 27, 1910 in the city of Skopje (now capital of the *Republic of Macedonia*) in erstwhile Yugoslavia. She was the third and last child born to her Albanian Catholic parents, Nikola and Dranafile Bojaxhiu. Nikola was a self-made, successful businessman and Dranafile stayed home to take care of the children.

When she was eight years old her father died in 1919. The Bojaxhiu family was

devastated. After a period of intense grief, her mother sold textiles and hand-made embroidery to bring in some income. She raised Agnes as a Roman Catholic.

Now the Bojaxhiu family held tightly to their religious beliefs. The family prayed daily and went on pilgrimages annually. In her early years Agnes was fascinated by stories of the lives of *missionaries* and their service in Bengal.

Childhood Intelligence

One day Agnes' mother saw her children playing with some dirty kids. She called her children, "Don't play with them. If you do you will become like them — unclean, uncultured and shabby."

Lazar and the elder daughter stood silent. But Agnes said, "Mom! Can't these bad kids be made good? You tell us the stories of the saints reforming evil ones into noble people. Similarly, those kids can be educated into civilized ones. Isn't that right?"

The mother looked at Agnes admiringly

and nodded her head saying, "You are right, my daughter. Our aim should be to help them and not to hate them."

The Call

When Agnes was 12 years old, she began to feel to serve God as a nun. Deciding to become a nun was a very difficult decision. Becoming a nun not only meant giving up the chance to marry and have children, it also meant giving up all her worldly possessions and her family, perhaps forever.

For five years, young Agnes thought very seriously whether or not to become a nun. During this time, she sang in the church choir, helped her mother to organize church events, and went on walks with her mother to hand out food to the poor.

When Mother Teresa was 17, she made the difficult decision to become a nun. Having read many articles about the work Catholic missionaries were doing in India, Mother Teresa was determined to go there. Thus, Mother Teresa applied to the Loreto order of nuns, based in Ireland but with missions in India.

Becoming a Nun

In September 1928, 18-year-old Agnes said goodbye to her family to travel to Ireland and then on to India. She joined the *Sisters of Loreto* as a missionary. After that she never saw her mother or sister again.

It took more than two years to become a Loreto nun. After spending six weeks in Ireland, learning the history of the Loreto order and to study English, the language the Sisters of Loreto used to teach school children in India. Mother Teresa then travelled to India, where she arrived on January 6, 1929.

After two years as a novice, Mother Teresa took her first vows as a Loreto nun on May 24, 1931.

As a new Loreto nun, Mother Teresa (known then only as Sister Teresa, a name she chose after St. Teresa of Lisieux, Spain) settled in to the Loreto Entally convent in Kolkata (previously called *Calcutta*) and began teaching history and geography at the convent schools.

In Indian Colours

Sister Teresa was born Christian and had come to India for service to the poor. The conditions of the hungry and half-naked poor made Teresa to give-up the costly dress of the mission and opt for the same simple dress as worn by the street cleaner women of the Calcutta municipality. Thus she identified herself with the poorest of the land.

Became Mother Teresa

Usually, Loreto nuns were not allowed to leave the convent; however, in 1935, 25-year-old Mother Teresa was given a special exemption to teach at a school outside of the convent, St. Teresa's. After two years at St. Teresa's, Mother Teresa took her final vows on May 24, 1937 and officially became 'Mother Teresa'.

Almost immediately after taking her final vows, Mother Teresa became the headmistress of St. Mary's, one of the convent schools. She was once again restricted to live within the convent's walls. She served there for almost twenty years.

Although Teresa enjoyed teaching at the school, she was increasingly disturbed by the poverty surrounding her in Calcutta. The *Bengal famine of 1943* brought misery and death to the city; and the outbreak of *Hindu-Muslim violence in August 1946* plunged the city into despair and horror.

Blessed Blue Bordered Sari

On the evening of August 16, 1946 Mother Teresa removed her old religious dress and wore a new dress of her future *Missionary of Charity Order*. Her new dress consisted of a simple, cotton, white sari with blue stripes (blue was the colour of Virgin Mary) alongwith white dress to be worn under the sari.

Mother Teresa had adopted Indian citizenship in 1948. She was an Indian to the core of her heart. She wore like an Indian and ate Indian food. While starting her *Missionaries of Charity* she had to select a dress for the missionaries. Calcutta municipal street sweeper women used to wear blue bordered sari as uniform. Mother opted for that dress.

Mother Teresa took the dress to the Father and prayed to him to bless it. Father said, "Sister! Do you know that it is the uniform that the lowest of the municipal workers wear? And the people here consider them untouchables."

Mother said, "For me that is the reason for choosing it. I want to be identified with the

lowest and the poorest of this land. My mission is to sweep away the woes, pains and neglect of the poor and sick."

There were tears in Father's eyes. He bent down with Mother Teresa and prayed to God before blessing the pair of blue bordered saris.

Indian by Choice

In 1946, Mother Teresa was doing the ground work for starting her own *Missionaries of Charity*. She was staying in a room at the third floor of the house owned Michael Gomez. In the name of possessions she only had a wooden box and a framed picture of Virgin Mary. She used to sleep on a mat. Being penniless even the food was a problem. The kind Gomez family helped her as far as they could.

Once, Mother Teresa was travelling in a Tram in Calcutta. Some people stared at Mother Teresa. For them a white woman travelling in a Tram is not a common sight. The people were whispering. Some had very weird fears. A man asked mother her nationality. Mother replied that she is an

Indian. Another onlooker said how could a white skinned claimed as an Indian. Mother promptly replied that you people are Indian by accident but I am Indian by choice.

Swiss Man's Ego Punctured

Mother Teresa was critical of western people running down India for its poverty and illiteracy. For her India was her country and its honour her own.

Once, a Swiss businessman came to see Mother. He owned many companies and proud of his riches.

When he met Mother he said, "Mother, you don't know how rich I am. I give charity to so many missionaries. When I heard about poverty of Indians I came here to help people. I can finance several homes like this one which you are running. I want to do charity here through you."

Mother Teresa didn't like his way of talking. She said, "If you have so much money to spare you should open shelters for the poor of your country. Where people like

you live then most of the others are bound to be poor. My country India is poor but we have generous enough people here who can help me open homes in even the rich countries."

Mother's plane talk punctured the ego bubble of the rich Swiss.

Help to Needy

A school established by Mother at Moti Jheel transformed the slum children into neat and well mannered kids. Enthused with this success slum dwellers collect one hundred rupees for Mother. With that money she rented two rooms at Rs. 5 each. One room served as her school and the other room as a clinic for the sick.

The hard work put in by Mother earned the praise of the others. A sister volunteered to teach the children and one other tended the sick. Mother would meet people to know their problems and tried to work out answers. The slum dwellers were always being harassed by the authorities.

Feeling Pain of Poor

One day Mother Teresa was out in streets of Calcutta. It was cold. Suddenly she saw a woman and her child shivering in a broken and without roof hut. Mother touched the child, it was running with fever. A torn saree was on the woman's body. It shocked Mother.

She asked the woman about the reason for her such a pathetic condition.

The woman sobbed and revealed, "Hut rent was not paid for the last two months. The landlord took away the roof. If I leave this hut the landlord would take possession of it. How can I leave this hut? I have nowhere to go."

Mother Teresa comforted her and took her to Moti Jheel clinic to provide her the shelter.

Meeting Jawaharlal Nehru

India became independent on 15th August, 1947 and Jawahar Lal Nehru took oath as its first Prime Minister.

It was winter of 1947. Mother Teresa was celebrating X-mas in a government school. The Chief Minister of West Bengal was to be the chief guest. Co-incidentally Jawaharlal Nehru happened to be in Calcutta on that day. He came to know about celebration and sent a message that he too wanted to attend her party.

Mother Teresa replied that it would be a privilege for her to have him as a guest and said that the poor kids would be delighted to find him with them.

Nehru arrived there and warmly welcomed by Mother and children. Nehru praised the work and efforts put by mother for the downtrodden of the society. He found no words to correctly praise the selfless service being rendered by Mother Teresa.

Home for Lepers

In 1950, the relatives of a woman left her at the door of *Mother Home*. She was wearing costly ornaments. As she was suffering from leprosy, her rich sons were not ready to keep her with them. Mother sheltered her. But the other patients of the Home were uneasy about her presence by their side.

Mother had noticed a lot of such abandoned lepers lying by the road sides having no shelter or care. For them Mother set up a Leper Home in Teetagarh where Sisters went twice a week to give medicines.

When that rich woman came to know the reality she declared her wish to dedicate her life to the mission of Mother Teresa. At Teetagarh a separate home for female lepers came up and that woman was shifted to it. She lived there helping other patients true to her word.

Determined Mother Teresa

Once, Mother Teresa saw a woman dying on the footpath. She took the woman to a nearby hospital loaded on a rickshaw. At the hospital she was told that no bed was vacant.

Mother pleaded with the hospital staff to admit that dying woman somehow.

The doctor said, "The woman is dying. Take her away."

Mother insisted, "But she is still alive. How can we let her die. She needs immediate attention to stay alive. Please do something."

The doctor was an arrogant one, he said, "We don't have time to waste on her," and went to his cabin.

Mother Teresa sat down on the floor with that sick woman in her lap. After some time the doctor emerged out of his cabin to go home. He found Mother sitting there. The doctor's conscience bit him. He examined the woman and gave treatment. At last, the woman survived.

Mother Praised by Nehru

It was year 1960. Despite of his illness, Nehru inaugurated a *Mother Home*. Mother Teresa wanted to brief him about her organisation *Missionaries of Charity*.

Nehru replied, "Mother, no need for that. It does not require any introduction. All the people know about your work. The entire world is indebted to you for your services to the abandoned, orphans and the hapless sick people. The dedication of your mission is matchless. Your patience and selfless devotion is incredible." Those words overwhelmed Mother Teresa. Tears rolled off her eyes.

Nirmal Hriday

Mother Teresa used to see several critically ill patients lying on the roadside without any one caring for them. Mother decided to do something about it to give the dying a graceful death. She needed a place to open a home for the critically ill.

She went to the municipal corporation

office and met an official of the health department. The officer was a kind and considerate man. He told Mother about a place near Kalighat temple. It was a *dharmashala* captured by some anti-social elements. Mother decided to use that place for her social service work.

That *dharmashala* consisted of two large halls. Mother and her volunteers started bringing in terminally sick patients from the roadsides. Dedicated Sisters of the Mission began to tend the sick. That home was named *Nirmal Hridaya* (Pious Heart) by Mother.

That Crippled Girl

In many other cities of India *Mother Homes* were coming up. One under construction was in Jaipur. Mother had gone there to inspect it. While going to Church for her evening prayers she saw a crippled orphan girl dragging her paralysed legs on the road pathetically.

Mother felt pity for the girl and went to her. She enquired about her parents. The girl replied, "No parents and no brother-sister.

They left me because I am a cripple. I beg on roads."

Her talk amused Mother. She took her into Home and was given new clothes to wear. A Sister informed the girl, "Now onwards, you will live here with us."

Chemistry with Indira Gandhi

It was time when Indira Gandhi was the Prime Minister of India. She had great respect and love for Mother. Whenever Mother was out of the country Indira Gandhi used to keep track of the welfare of Mother's Home. Once, Delhi Home for orphans ran out of pulses and vegetables. The Sisters were in a fix. When Indira Gandhi came to know about it she made immediate arrangements. A tempo loaded with fresh vegetables from her kitchen garden arrived at the Home.

Mother Teresa and Indira Gandhi had a special chemistry. Once Mother fell seriously ill and Indira Gandhi flew to see her leaving behind her busy schedule to Darjeeling where Mother was under intensive care in a nursing home.

Homes Abroad

The fame of the *Missionaries of Charity* brought many requests and offers to Mother Teresa for opening Homes abroad. But Mother had to refuse as she was short of Sisters to work abroad.

At the insistence of Pope John Paul-II Mother opened her first overseas Home in Venezuela. Pope had visited India just for that purpose. Mother's work had so impressed him that he gifted her Ford Lincoln luxury car specially airlifted to India for his tour.

Mother Teresa and her Sisters went to the war zones to offer their services to the injured even at the cost of the danger to their lives.

Once Mother went to Ethiopia that suffered from a severe famine. The people were dying of starvation. Emperor Haile Selassie of that country was a ruthless Muslim fanatic. Yet Mother was able to convince him that her work was above narrow politics or religion.

Mother opened Haile Selassie Missionaries of Charity and saved the starvation ravaged sick people in large numbers.

In 1987, Mother opened 'Tuman Home' in Philippines for the people suffering from T.B. The home was situated in slum colony of the poorest in the capital city of Manila. That was another Asian country suffering from abject poverty and diseases.

Cleanest & Pious

In 1971 Indo-Pak war the Pakistani army let loose a reign of terror in East Pakistan forcing millions of people to flee to India to take refuge.

Mother had her camps at Calcutta to help the sick refugees. The refugees were living in a tent city created by the government and many voluntary organizations. American Senator, Edward Kennedy, came to India to see the condition of the refugee camps.

Edward Kennedy entered a camp run by Missionaries of Charity. He saw a Sister cleaning the wounds of a patient. Senator

moved forward with extended hand wanting to shake the hands of Sister. Sister withdrew her hands and stammered, "Sir, my hands are dirty."

Edward Kennedy remarked, "Sister, there cannot be anything more clean and pious than your hands." He grabbed Sister's hand with both of his own and shook warmly.

Coconut Shell

Once, Mother saw two boys fighting. Mother asked them why they were fighting. Boys revealed that the bone of contention was the coconut shell.

Mother was surprised. She saw a lot of shells lying around. The boys didn't pick them but fighting for a particular one?

When enquired boys revealed that the shell had coconut water inside. Others were empty ones. The fight was for the water the shell contained.

Instantly an idea struck the Mother mind. Why not employ the kids in the job of collecting shells? The shells could yield coconut jute for making mats, door mats and ropes.

But the problem was, where to store all the shells? Mother had no godown. She tried and in 1973 she managed to get a space in Sialdah as a donation. Mother decided to turn it into a Home.

Premdaan

Mother named her new venture Premdaan. She spread the message around that, the boys bringing in 100 coconut shells each, would get a treat of butter and bread slices. It created a wave among the street urchins and a competition to collect waste shells began.

The people used to drink coconut water and the shells were thrown near coconut stalls. Thus shells used to be all around as uncared for waste. The kids would make 100-shell bags and Mother's Home truck would drive around to collect the bags in exchange for bread and butter.

Premdaan later turned into a big Home where homeless old men, handicapped and orphans were sheltered. It is still in business. The inmates are taught to make ropes, mats, bags etc. out of coconut jute to earn a living.

Singapore Incident

Once, Mother Teresa happened to visit Singapore. There, a sixteen year old beautiful girl met her and wished to join her mission. She had a younger brother who was physical challenged. She told mother, "My brother's head is very big making him look like a monster. Everyone hates and laughs at him. But I like him because he is my brother. What should I do?"

Mother said, "My child, love God. Those who don't sympathise with handicapped ones, God does not love them. You must love all handicapped people. The doors of my Home are open for you. Dedicate your life to the service of the suffering. I will send you and your brother to my Home situated in Siboo town."

The young girl had got what she always prayed for. She became a part of Mother's mission and went to Siboo in Philippines. Her deformed brother also was happy in the Home where no one despised or laughed at him.

No to Custom Duty

The Homes established by Mother Teresa got huge donations from all over the world. Most of the rich Western countries used to send drugs as donations for Mother's Homes.

Once two sisters came to Mother and reported, "Mother! The custom people are not releasing the drug consignments sent to us as donations. They want tax."

Mother firmly said, "Why we pay custom duty? We don't take anything from the government for our Homes? These drugs are not for profit making. They are given free to the needy of this very country. These consignments are donated by kind people of many countries. Why tax them? I am determined that we shall pay no tax on the donations we receive."

It happened in Philippines. A helpful Indian who was Mother's confidant approached the concerned minister and pleaded Mother's case. The minister had to make the consignments delivered to Mother's Homes.

Old Age Homes

Mother had set up Homes for the poor, sick and the orphans. Later she set up Homes for the abandoned old people too.

In Hong Kong, a rich old age Japanese

couple committed suicide in their flat. Their sons and daughters had abandoned them. They had written in the suicide note—"We are unable to look after ourselves. So, we have decided to die. Our flat be sold and half of the money be given to Mother Teresa for her 'Old Age Home' and the other half be donated to the other charities serving the old people."

When Mother came to know about this sad incident she at once took a decision to open 'Old Age Homes' in rich countries where old people suffered from the neglect by their children.

A Living Legend

Everywhere she went, stories would emerge, legends would grow. How as a young sister she offered to work her own passage abroad as an air hostess; how she would tell air hostesses to pack up left-over food in a bag for children; how she asked the Nobel prize organisers to cancel the traditional banquet and use the money to feed children. Perhaps because she was in a way the conscience of an apathetic world, because she made up for everyone else's inaction, no one dared shut the door in her face.

The prime minister of Yemen, for instance, impressed by her work, lifted a 600-year-old ban on Christian missionaries in the 1960s and invited her into his country. Though barely 5 ft at tiptoe, the rich, the famous, the powerful were dwarfed by her. Edward Kennedy wept in public; Indira Gandhi, out of power in 1978, found time in her hectic schedule to meet her; no one dared argue when she walked through the still-smouldering streets of West Beirut leading a group of orphaned children to their new home.

The respect she earned was paid back through a heap of awards. *The Nobel Peace* — Pope John Paul honoured her with 'Peace Prize'.

— USA gave her *'Kennedy International Award'*.

— In 1980, the government of India conferred on her the country's highest civilian award — *'Bharat Ratna'*.

Mother Teresa felt very embarrassed in the glittering ceremonies arranged to honour her.

She attended all the functions in her humble blue bordered sari.

Mother's Prayer

Mother had never met Gandhiji but had great respect and love for him. She had named her Home for lepers as *Gandhiji Prem Niwas.*

Mother used to sit with the lepers and pray —

'O Lord God! Enable me to serve the poor and the sick. Help me to feed the hungry and give medicine to the diseased. Let my hands feed all those who are hungry. Fill me with love to create peace for all. God, send me as a messenger of peace among those who are hateful. Let me turn their hatred into love. Give me power to bring justice where there is injustice, peace where there is unrest, get the strayed ones on right path, faith into faithless hearts, hope where there is no hope and light where there is darkness. O God, fill my life with light to help me fill the lives of unfortunate ones with the light of happiness.'

Mother was the one person who practiced what she preached.

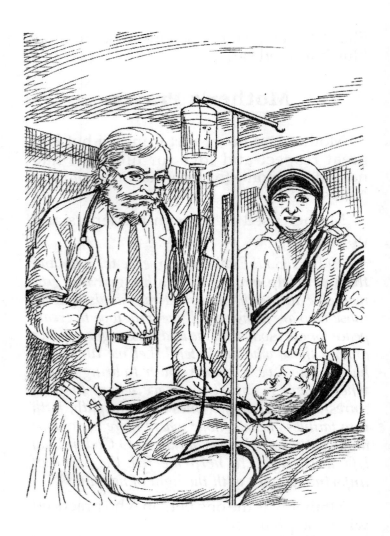

The Last Voyage

Mother was not keeping well as she grew older and taxed her body with over work. In 1996, she resigned from the chief post of her organization.

Sister Nirmala took over the charge.

Her resignation became a worldwide news. Many had the feeling that Mother Teresa had sensed her fast approaching end.

In September 1996, her condition worsened. On doctor's advice she was admitted to ICU of a hospital in Kolkata. She had grown very weak. 10th December was the day she had founded her 'Missionaries of Charity' almost a half century ago. Every year she celebrated that day as *Inspiration Day*.

Inspite of serious condition she attended the function and said that she might not be there in the following year's celebration. Mother asked the Sisters to continue the service work regardless.

For eight months Mother Teresa struggled with the death. Then, on 5th September, 1997

Mother felt a surge of excruciating pain in her frail body. Her body collapsed, never to breathe again.

The news plunged the world in grief and homages started pouring in.

On 13th September, 1997 Mother Teresa was given burial with full state honours. Such honour to a civilian was accorded to the other person only — Mahatma Gandhi.

Missionaries of Charity after Mother Teresa

Sister Nirmala succeeded Mother Teresa as leader of the Missionaries of Charity in March of 1997. Undaunted by the prospect of following in the footsteps of Mother Teresa, she has said, "I have to walk in my own shoes. We will continue as we have been doing."

Sister Nirmala was a Hindu until the age of 24, when, inspired by Mother Teresa's service to the poor, she converted to Catholicism. She took as her religious name a Hindi word that suggests a purity of mind and spirit.

Sister Nirmala has a master's degree in political science from an Indian university and additional training as a lawyer. She headed missions in Panama, Europe, and in Washington D.C., before being chosen to succeed Mother Teresa.

The Missionaries of Charity reach out to the poorest of poor, taking in the destitute and the dying, bathing their wounds and helping those about to pass on, to do so with dignity.

Mother Teresa Memorial House

The Mother Teresa Memorial House is dedicated to the *humanitarian* and *Nobel Peace Prize* laureate *Mother Teresa* and is located in her hometown *Skopje*, in the *Republic of Macedonia*. The memorial house was built on the popular Macedonia Street in the *Centar municipality*, on the very location of the once Sacred Heart of Jesus Roman Catholic Church, where Mother Teresa was baptized.

The memorial house, worth two million Euro was opened on 30th January 2009 by *Macedonian Prime Minister*. The opening was attended by foreign delegations, members of the *Roman Catholic Church in Macedonia* and *Macedonian Orthodox Church*. One week prior to the opening, the Macedonian Foreign Minister placed a commemorative plate at Mother Teresa's grave in *Kolkata*, with the engravement *"Token of Gratitude from the Republic of Macedonia and the Fellow-Citizens of Her Native Town Skopje."*

The construction of the house began in May 2008. The project was financed by the Government of the Republic of Macedonia and carried out by the Ministry of Culture. It is a modern, transformed version of Mother Teresa's birth house and has a multifunctional, but sacral character. Inside the house, part of her relics are preserved, which have been transferred to Skopje with support of the *Roman Catholic Church* of Skopje.

There is a museum and sculptures of Mother Teresa and the members of her family in realistic appearance. One sculpture shows

Mother Teresa as a ten-year old child, sitting on a stone and holding a pigeon in her hands.

Sainthood of Mother Teresa

The beatification of Mother Teresa was conducted in October 19, 2003 by Pope John Paul II. Pope John Paul II beatified Mother Teresa, who died in 1997. The beatification of the Macedonia-born nun took place in Rome, and her popularity has remained strong in the months since.

The process leading up to the beatification has been the shortest in modern history. In early 1999 — less than two years after Mother Teresa's death — Pope John Paul waived the normal five-year waiting period and allowed the immediate opening of her canonization cause.

In 2002, the Holy Father recognized the healing of an Indian woman as the miracle needed to beatify Mother Teresa of Calcutta. That healing occurred on the first anniversary of Mother Teresa's death. It involved a non-Christian woman in India who had a huge abdominal tumour and woke up to find the tumour gone. Members of the Missionaries of Charity prayed for their founder's intervention to help the sick woman.

"Her life of loving service to the poor has inspired many to follow the same path. Her witness and messages are cherished by those of every religion as a sign that 'God still loves the world today," members of the Missionaries of Charity, the religious order she founded, said in a statement after Mother Teresa's beatification was announced.

Since her death, they said, "People have sought her help and have experienced God's love for them through her prayers. Every day, pilgrims from India and around the world come to pray at her tomb, and many more follow her example of humble service of love to the most needy, beginning in their own families."

In 2001, on the Feast of the Assumption of Mary, officials closed the diocesan inquiry into Mother Teresa's sanctity. The year-long gathering of testimony from those who knew Mother Teresa was the first major step in a typically long process. A year earlier, at an

August 26, 2000, celebration in Calcutta marking Mother Teresa's birth anniversary, Hindu, Sikh and Muslim admirers joined in common prayers for her speedy canonization.

A second *miracle* is required for her to proceed to *canonization.*

Timeline : Mother Teresa

Aug 27, 1910   Born as Agnes Gonxa Bojaxhiu in Skopje in the former Yugoslavia.

1928   Becomes Roman Catholic Loreto nun and begins training in Loreto Abbey, Dublin, Ireland, takes name Sister Teresa.

1929   Arrives in Calcutta, India, becomes a teacher at St. Mary's High School.

1937   Takes final vows as a nun.

1948   Permitted to leave order and moves to slums to start school.

1948	Transfers her citizenship from Yugoslavia to India. Left the convent to work alone in the slums. Receives *medical* training in Paris.
1950	Founds the Missionaries of Charity.
1952	Opens Nirmal Hriday (Pure Heart), home for the dying.
1953	Opens orphanage.
1957	Begins her work with lepers for which her order becomes well known around the world.
1958	Order's first facility outside of Calcutta opens in Drachi, India.
1962	Wins first prize for work among the poor: Padma Shri award.
1965	The Catholic *Church grants* the order permission

to organize missions outside of India.

1971 Receives the Pope John XXIII Peace Prize and uses the $25,000 to build a leper colony.

1979 Awarded Nobel Peace Prize for work with destitute and dying.

1982 Persuades the Israelis and Palestinians to cease fire long enough to rescue 37 retarded children from Beirut.

1983 Has heart attack while visiting Pope John Paul II.

1985 Awarded 'Medal of Freedom'.

1989 Suffers second heart attack, fitted with pacemaker.

1990 Re-elected superior general of her order of the Missionaries for Charity, despite her wish to step down.

1992	Enters the hospital in *La Jolla*, Californiafor treatment of pneumonia and congestive heart failure.
1993	Falls and breaks three ribs in May, hospitalized for malaria in August, undergoes surgery for blocked blood vessel in September.
1996	Falls and breaks collarbone in April, suffers malarial fever and left ventricle failure in August, receives honorary citizenship on November sixteenth.
March 13, 1997	Steps down as the head of her order, is succeeded by Sister Nirnala.
Sept. 5, 1997	Dies of a massive heart attack in Calcutta at the age of 87.

Poems of Mother Teresa

"People are often unreasonable and self-centered. Forgive them anyway.

If you are kind, people may accuse you of ulterior motives. Be kind anyway.

If you are honest, people may cheat you. Be honest anyway.

If you find happiness, people may be jealous. Be happy anyway.

The good you do today may be forgotten tomorrow. Do good anyway.

Give the world the best you have and it may never be enough. Give your best anyway.

For you see, in the end, it is between you and God. It was never between you and them anyway."

"Life is an opportunity, benefit from it.

Life is beauty, admire it.

Life is a dream, realize it.

Life is a challenge, meet it.

Life is a duty, complete it.

Life is a game, play it.

Life is a promise, fulfill it.

Life is sorrow, overcome it.

Life is a song, sing it.

Life is a struggle, accept it.

Life is a tragedy, confront it.

Life is an adventure, dare it.

Life is luck, make it.

Life is too precious, do not destroy it.

Life is life, fight for it."

"If you are kind, people may accuse you of selfish, ulterior motives; be kind anyway.

If you are successful, you will win some false friends and true enemies; succeed anyway.

If you are honest and frank, people may cheat you; be honest and frank anyway.

If you find serenity and happiness, they may be jealous; be happy anyway.

The good you do today, people will often forget tomorrow; do good anyway...

You see, in the final analysis, it is between you and God; it was never between you and them anyway."

❑ ❑ ❑